For Mike Secomins who is immersed in the Ocean of experience. Pat ... 2/30/

TALKING

WITH

BIRCHES

Also by Pat Parnell:

*Snake Woman and Other Explorations, Finding
the Female in Divinity.* Poems, 2001.

TALKING WITH BIRCHES

I share the best
thing I can make—this stitching
together of memory

and heart-scrap

Wesley McNair, "Reading Poems at the
Grange Meeting in What Must Be Heaven"
My Brother Running

POEMS OF FAMILY
AND EVERYDAY LIFE

Pat Parnell

The Journal Press, Inc.

Acknowledgments

I would like to thank the editors of the following publications in which earlier versions of these poems originally appeared: *Cadence; Corpus Reports; Exeter (N.H.) Newsletter; Garden Lane; Issue #7; Journal; Journal of the Northern Virginia Writing Project; Kettle of Fish; Maine Times; New Hampshire College Journal; Northern New England Review; Poetry Vending Machine; Poet's Touchstone; Portfolio; Re-Imagining; White Pines College Alumni Newsletter; White Pines College Yearbook; Wordplay; Worcester Review; www.bentspoon.net.*

Anthologies: *Anthology of New England Writers, 2001; Currents II; Love and Trouble; Summer of '78; True Stories, Guides for Writing from Your Life.* CD: *Esther Buffler and Friends—High on Poetry.*

"Dark Necessity" appeared in a longer version in *Snake Woman and Other Explorations, Finding the Female in Divinity.*

Photographs of birches by Debi Wheeler-Bean, Exeter, N. H.

The photograph of Sanyu Mande (p. 73) first appeared in the 1989 and 1990 yearbooks of White Pines College, now Chester College of New England. Used with permission.

Copyright 2004 by Pat Parnell
Printed and bound in the United States of America

Publisher: The Journal Press, Inc. P. O. 409, King George, VA 22485
Distributed by Enfield Books, P. O. 699, Enfield, NH 03748

ISBN 0-9746111-0-7   LCCN 2004092802

For my sister, Ruth Herrink, and my cousins, Carol Cole and Ellen Machamer, and for all our extended families, that we may remember and share the family stories and cherish the richness of family.

Many Thanks

To my careful and astute readers, Muriel Stubbs, Karen Galipeau, and Mike Albert, for their discerning analyses. Any lack of felicity is mine, not theirs. And to Mary Gildea, for her careful proof-reading, including the spelling of BARBARA FRIETCHIE.

To my fellow writing group members and other writer friends for their careful vision and invaluable help.

To Richard Haynes and Carol Guba, for their inspired help with the photographs.

To Wesley McNair, who first told me I had to preserve my family stories.

And to Cicely Buckley, who nudged me into telling them in *Talking with Birches*.

Table of Contents

Art

Talking with Birches

Our father and mother, Basil and Ruth Jones, both loved a good story. On summer evenings on our screened porch in Richmond, Virginia, Daddy would play his harmonica, sing some of his favorite songs ("O, we're going to the Hamburg show...") and tell stories of growing up in Danville, Virginia, on the cusp of the 20th century. A man of the highest personal and professional integrity, he also relished the ribald and the raunchy in song and story. From his college and medical school days, he had a scatological repertoire which he might perform for us, always with the most risque parts censored. My sister and I had fun trying to fill in the blanks. He loved limericks, especially those on the shady side ("There was a young man from New Kent..."). In his last illness, when he could no longer speak, he could still laugh. Our son Ed would read to him from a favorite collection of Ozark folk tales, *Pissing in the Snow*, with Grandpa chuckling in accompaniment. Daddy's sense of humor echoes through these pages as it still echoes through our family life.

Mother, a social worker, entertained every evening at dinner with dramatic versions of the day's events or tales of her childhood in Geneva, New York, and Portsmouth, New Hampshire. Her mother, she told us, recited poetry while ironing, and our mother had her own repertoire of poems she knew by heart ("It was the schooner Hesperus, that sailed the wintry sea..."). Our parents, Yankee and Southerner, sometimes refought the Civil War with Mother's highly emotional recitation of "Barbara Frietchie" ("Shoot if you must, this old gray head...").

They shared a passion for gardening. Long before anyone ever dreamed of Earth Day, they were organic gardeners, complete with compost pile and mulch. Beginning in the early 1930s, they took the barren red clay city lots on either side of our Richmond home and made fertile garden plots from them, rich brown crumbly earth.

Some of Mother's liveliest stories came from their gardening experiences. According to one story, which she relished recounting, she had read about the advantages of earthworms in the compost pile, so she ordered a batch of them. The box arrived with one corner crushed in shipping. The worms looked healthy and vigorous, but the directions in the package said to report any damage to postal authorities. The next day, she took her lunch hour and went to the nearest post office. When she told the clerk she had received a package that was damaged in the mail, he asked, "What was in the package, ma'am?"

"One thousand worms."

The clerk thought for a few seconds. Then he said, "Well, ma'am, you go home and count those worms. And if any are missing, you fill out a report and we'll take care of it."

Of course, she just dumped the box into the compost pile without counting, but gaining a good story to tell more than made up for the few worms that might have escaped in transit.

Although Mother was born in Geneva, she moved with her family to Portsmouth when she was about eleven. In spite of her years in Virginia after her marriage, the Granite State was always home to her. She and our father came to visit for a couple of weeks every summer while my sister and I were spending our school vacations at our grandparents' cottage at Wallis Sands Beach, Rye, New Hampshire. One of her deepest regrets, when she could no longer travel, was "I'll never see New Hampshire again!"

White birches, the official state tree, symbolized New Hampshire to her. To bring a little of New Hampshire to her Richmond home, Mother planted a clump of birch trees on the front lawn. The birches gave Mother another story that she cherished.

The time was the early 1960s, with the beginnings of the environmental movement, and Mother had found a book on talking to plants. Daddy, a doctor with a scientist's point of view, pooh-pooh'd the whole idea. Our son Bill used that book later for a high school science fair project, and he still claims he proved that talking to plants made a difference in their growth.

To make those transplanted New England trees feel good about being in the South, Mother said, she used to stop on the front walk and talk with them every morning on her way to work. She told them how beautiful they were and how much she enjoyed having them in her yard. She chatted with them about family history and the latest family news, regaling them with her favorite stories. After a while, she claimed, "I noticed that the parts of the cluster that were nearest the sidewalk were flourishing, the trunks were getting taller and stronger, and the branches were full of green leaves. They seemed to feel at home." But on the far side, she said, the trunks were still thin and spindly and the leaves were sparse. "They felt ignored. They didn't think I was talking to them."

So Mother began walking all around the birches every morning, talking to every part. Although our father kept on kidding her, she would not be deterred from her nurturing. "And sure enough," she used to say, "the spindly trunks began to get stronger and fill out and the leaves got thicker and greener."

Whatever magic she used, the birches flourished. They are tall and white and strong today. I believe something of her caring spirit still watches over them.

As I began to gather the poems for this book, I remembered the birches and the family stories. Think of these poems, not as complete family history but as mini-memoirs, bits of family gossip, "memory and heart-scrap," in poet Wesley McNair's phrase. Stories exchanged over the dinner table in lingering conversation after a meal. Brightening the darkness of a warm Virginia evening. Or shared in rocking chairs on the front porch of the Wallis Sands cottage as we relaxed in the ocean breezes, chatting over crochet, knitting, and needlepoint. Or with Mother on a morning walk around the front yard, talking with birches.

Slowly, ever so slowly
the words drift into the room
like cobwebs and fill it
with shapes and shadows
that filter sunlight and give
a chance to unprotected memory.
DOLORES KENDRICK, "Pieces of the Past"
Why the Woman is Singing on the Corner

Miriam

1868-1959

My father's mother
was raised a Victorian lady
in an era that put lacy pantaloons
on piano limbs.
No bare legs
in those parlors.

One Sunday morning
my sister and I were plopped
on the living room rug—
pajamas, bathrobes,
and fuzzy slippers—
reading the comics.

Visiting for the weekend,
Grandmother came downstairs
dressed in her Sunday best.
"My father (her most Victorian voice)
never saw me in my nightclothes.
Except once.

I was very young. And very ill. In bed.
He came into my room
to ask how I was feeling.
I was so embarrassed.
I hid under the covers.
I couldn't answer him."

Minnie Seybolt Redner

Min
1863-1947

Great-aunt Minnie
was the only girl
in a family of three brothers.
She bragged, "My father
always said
I was the best boy he had."

In her first pregnancy,
the doctor came drunk, fumbling,
to the childbirth.
(My mother and my aunts
would whisper this story.)
The baby died. For the rest of Min's life,
we learned after her funeral,
her womb hung between her thighs
like a flaccid penis.

Min ran a canning factory, doing a man's job,
bossing the women who packed tomatoes,
corn, carrots, peas, green beans
brought by wagonload from the nearby fields.

"I believe in love,"
she would say when we visited,
leaning forward in her rocker
to stab her cane at us.
"Loving everybody. Not the kind of love
you go to bed with."

She offered a college education,
all expenses paid,
to any grandniece named for her.
None of us bears her name:
Minerva Augusta.

Lizzie

1871- 1964

When my Great-aunt Lizzie was a little girl,
her great-aunt lay dying
in the spare room of the family home.
Consumption.

Lizzie was her companion, Auntie's little helper.
Bringing fresh water,
clean handkerchiefs.
Playing quietly with her dolls
on the Turkey-red carpet by the sickbed.

Auntie had a hot toddy every afternoon
to ease her pain.
Because Lizzie was so good,
Auntie always gave her a treat.

Every day
Lizzie finished the sugar and the whiskey
at the bottom of Auntie's glass,

using Auntie's spoon.

Cora

1864-1939

I. Sunday Afternoons

Great-aunt Cora tipped tables.

Born a Lafferty, she brought into the family her dark Celtic mysticism. Our own Shanachie, she found death in dreams, told tales of ghosts and poltergeists. Communed with spirits: Ouija, planchette, tipping tables. One tip for yes, two for no.

It's the mid-1930's. Our living room houses the perfect tipping table: cherry, top 15 inches across, raised rim. Center pedestal with three curved feet. On Sunday afternoon visits, Cora draws the blinds, squeezes all available children with her around the table, only our fingertips touching the surface. In the semi-darkness, we cross thumbs, link fifth fingers to form an unbroken circle.

Silence. No one moving. Tingles run up our fingers, tickle wrists and arms. The table moves slightly, rises on one side, settles back. "Do you want to talk with us?" Cora is whispering. One tip. Yes. "Are you a spirit?" Yes. "A good spirit?" Yes.

I watch Cora's hands as the table moves. White blotches on her fingertips tell me she's pushing. I can do better. After a break, I start pulling sideways with my hidden bottom thumb, all other fingers relaxed, touching lightly.

"You're cheating!" My sister. "No, I'm not," wiggling my fingers. The table stays tipped. Cora just smiles.

Once she told us a story someone had told her. A party where guests are table-tipping. A young man who stays aloof, mocking the idea of communing with spirits. The table begins to move toward him, rocking on its legs. As he jerks away, the table follows, so fast that most of the tippers drop off. Only one girl, laughing, keeps her fingers on the table as it chases the young man around the room. Finally he jumps behind a sofa, and the table gives up, after trying in vain to climb up on the cushions.

I still can't figure out how the girl made this work!

(A planchette is a small, thin, triangular board with rounded pegs at the two bottom corners and a hole for a pencil at the top. Great-aunt Cora, fascinated by the supernatural, used a planchette to try to reach the spirit world. She could work with it on her own, whenever the spirit moved her, and it is faster than the Ouija board, writing out words instead of spelling them letter by letter.
When our father was in medical school, just before World War I, he visited his Aunt Cora and Uncle Charlie whenever he had a free day. Cora loved telling stories of her contacts with the supernatural. Although he was a doctor, a man of science, and an agnostic in religion, skeptical of anything relating to the spiritual, our father relished her tales and enjoyed re-telling them.)

II. Cora and the Planchette

Imagine Aunt Cora, in stiff Victorian velveteen, sitting at a small table in front of an open fire in their study on a winter Sunday afternoon. Uncle Charlie sits near a window, smoking, reading a book from their collection. Perhaps the one which, in visits years later, so fascinated our father: *Demon Possession and Allied Themes*.

Cora's fingertips rest lightly on a planchette placed on a pad of notepaper. Her thumbs and first fingers are linked on the center; the other fingers rest lightly on the board. Electricity rises into her hands, prickling her wrists, her arms. The planchette begins to move, aimlessly, tracing a faint line over the paper. She keeps her fingers relaxed, letting the planchette move itself.

"Do you wish to communicate with me?" "Yes." The writing is clearer now. "Are you a spirit?" "No." "Are you human?" "Yes." "Are you alive or dead?" "Alive."

Imagine Cora's excitement. Her family and friends scoff at her attempts to reach the spirit realm. If she can contact this person.... "What is your name?" The planchette writes a name. "Where do you live?" "Rose Hill, Oklahoma."

The writing begins to trail off, and Cora has no more responses to her questions. Quickly she takes pen and notepaper, writes a letter to the postmaster at Rose Hill, Oklahoma. Without mentioning the spirit message, she tells him the name of her correspondent and asks if he knows of this person.

The answer comes back in a couple of weeks. "Yes," the postmaster says, "there is someone in Rose Hill by that name. He is an inmate in the local insane asylum and is in a deep coma. He is unable to communicate with anyone."

*   *   *

On another winter Sunday afternoon, sitting as before in front of the open fire, Cora is again experimenting with her planchette. Suddenly it begins to move wildly over the paper, making black, jagged marks.

"Are you a spirit?" **YES** Great dark letters. "Are you a good spirit or an evil spirit?" **EVIL** The writing larger, blacker, the vibrations in her hands and arms shaking her whole body. Cora throws the planchette into the fire and watches it burn.

"I never touched a planchette again."

Edward Seybolt
1861—1949

I am nine, walking with my grandfather
along the road behind the beach cottages.
It is August, and the afternoon sea-turn
has cooled the sultry day.

His favorites, black-eyed Susans, bloom
along the edge of our lot,
reflecting sunlight in their golden petals,
lifting their dark centers toward the sky.

Some of last year's seedheads still stand
on their dry stalks,
brown among the bright flowers.

With his bone-handled penknife
he has clipped a few of the faded circles,
dropped them in a pocket.

As we walk, he takes out two scratchy spheres,
hands one to me. Shows me how to roll it between
thumb and fingers, releasing the tiny seeds.
Farm-bred, he knows sowing.
His hand swings out. My hand follows.

The seeds scatter
beyond the edge of the pavement,
falling on the sandy soil
among the coarse beach grasses.

"Next summer," he says, "we will see our
black-eyed Susans blooming here."

One thing I was starting to understand was that August loved to tell a good story.

"Really, it's good for all of us to hear it again," she said. "Stories have to be told or they die, and when they die, we can't remember who we are or why we're here."

Cressie nodded, making the ostrich feathers wave through the air so you had the impression of a real bird in the room. "That's right. Tell the story, " she said.

SUE MONK KIDD, *The Secret Life of Bees*

Daddy and Patsy

We called him Daddy

for Basil B. Jones, M. D., 1892-1987

He had healing hands.

With gentle fingers
he would percuss a new-born's chest,
his other hand flat to cushion the soft thumping,
his stethoscope amplifying the unfolding lungs.

At his funeral, the minister told the story.
They were talking at the church coffee hour
when they heard crying from the nursery.
A mother brought in a screaming child, arm hanging at an angle.
Daddy softly touched the shoulder, seeing with his fingers,
then a quick movement, and the crying stopped,
mid-scream. The tear-streaked face looked up in awe,
wondering, the minister said, who this was who could
work miracles with his hands.

All growing things responded to his touch.
Thanks to his careful thumping and listening,
the watermelons and cantaloupes and honeydews he bought
were always ripe and juicy.
The young man next door says,
"He had the best garden in Richmond."
 All those years ago,
he and the other neighbor kids
watched for Daddy in the yard. He let them pick and eat.
Strawberries big as pingpong balls, bulging with sweetness.
Deep-purple blueberries they had to snatch
before the birds and squirrels gobbled them.
Raspberries and blackberries that left their fingers,
lips, tongues dyed with summer.

He loved to fish, his hands reading the fishing line
as they read a baby's chest. He felt the first tentative
nibble, waited just the right instant, and with a quick movement

had his quarry. Too small, and he would hold the fish
with wet hands, keeping it in the water,
release the hook, and set the youngster free.

His hands were his tools, always carefully cared for.
Once, in his last illness, I offered
to cut his fingernails. The long, straight fingers, blunt-ended,
still immaculate, with nails never that long.
I clipped carefully, trying not to pull or tear.
He was patient with my awkwardness.
When I finally finished, he tested each nail
with his thumb. One hand he could not move,
but he could test it with the other.
He could not speak,
but I knew, when he held out a finger,
what he meant.
I clipped again, until those hands
were perfect, as they had to be.

Doorways

Heading for the stairs, we passed an open door.

> Within the darkened room,
> shades drawn against the sun
> that summer Sunday afternoon
> almost sixty years ago,
> children lie crosswise on a big double bed,
> head to toe,
> as their ancestors lay
> in the holds of the slave ships.
> Age six or seven, they wear
> immaculate white dresses, lace ruffles at the hems,
> white trousers, white shirts, white ties.
> Lying perfectly still in the hot, airless room.
> Only the eyes move in the dark faces,
> watching us walk by.

We had come, my father and I, to visit Joe,
the neighborhood yard man, my mother's house man,
old and shrunken in his final illness.
Sitting in a white rocker in a white room,
his red and gray plaid shirt hanging off his shoulders,
his clean, faded khaki work pants, much too big for him now,
bunched at his waist like a brown paper bag.
Not the tall, sinewy man I remember from my childhood
when I watched in awe in the neighbor's yard,
seeing him grab a chicken behind its head,
swing it round and round in the air, and then give a jerk.
He laughed, watching us watch the chicken
as it ran in desperate circles, headless,
wings flapping, blood spurting from its neck,
until it dropped.

When we came back downstairs, the door was closed.

Blue Streak

My father loved to tell us girls this story:
How, in his Danville boyhood,
Virginia in the early 1900s,
he and his friends would hide in a barn,
clutching a handful of wooden matches.
One boy would strike a light,
and another would aim a blast
toward the flame.
Pale shining moons in the old barn's half-light
until the blue flame flared.

"Once," my father chuckled at the memory,
"one of the boys
let go such a mighty effort
that the blue flame flew back
and singed his cheeks.
And once I scorched my eyebrows,
twisting for a better view."

People say, "He talks a blue streak."
"She cursed a blue streak."
I never knew what blue streaks were,
until my father's tales.
How many who use the term
have ever seen a blue streak?
Have ever hidden in barn or basement
to experiment in its shadows?

Is this just a boy thing?

I can't imagine the proper little Danville girls
in that still-Victorian world
lifting their ruffled petticoats
to light up a dusky barn with their flames.

Spoor

As a child, in the 'Thirties,
she learned
to recognize poverty
by its smell.

Kerosene,
heating the linoleum-floored flat,
scenting the clothes,
of a school friend.

Stopping with her mother
to see a welfare client:
Sweet greasy fume
of cabbage simmering on the stove,
a slab of fatback cooking in it,
the meat for that night's supper.

Bringing a Christmas basket
to a third-floor tenement:
Thick sick stench of human dirt
bodies, hair
so heavy in the air that she could taste it.

In school, she sat next to a boy
whose ears smelled.

American Standard

"Always wipe the seat," my mother said,
crowding with me into the narrow stall,
"and put the paper down," showing me how.
"Although it may look clean," my mother said,
"you never know who has been there before."

Now, grown, I always do as Mother said—
Virtuous, obedient, sanitary—yet I
am the unknown to her who's next in line.
She will come after me to pause in fear
and wipe away the place where I have been.

Mother and Patsy

SeaDream Gift

for Ruth Seybolt Jones, 1898-1991

I walk along the edge of the waves, their last foam curling around my
    toes, swirling the sand, my ankles already stiff from the cold.
    The sun is warm through my big straw sunhat. I clutch a child's
    plastic bucket, pink fluorescent, with a pink metal shovel. I
    hope I look like a crazy old beach lady, walking to these New
    Hampshire rocks to collect shells. In the bucket is the black
    plastic box, half full.

Mother, I have left part of you with our father in the old green cemetery
    in Petersburg, Virginia, next to Great-uncle Theophilus and his
    niece Mamie, the baby who died. Corralled in plastic tube and
    bronze casing, you cannot escape to play the nurturing role you
    loved. You are preserved, waiting as you promised, waiting for
    the Last Day, the Trumpet, when you will rise and say, "Hi,
    Uncle Theophilus, I'm Ruth."

But part of you longs to be free, to return to this New Hampshire beach,
    to return to the world you loved. So you have come to me in
    this dream, walking with me, sitting with me as I sit on the cold
    wet seaweed of our favorite rocks, the brown stringy seaweed
    with the brown bubbles that pop like bubble wrap.

I lift the seaweed as if searching, my head bent, my back twisting away
    from the shore, hiding my hands. With the little pink shovel I
    scatter your ashes in the waves that surge around me. The flakes
    float like fish food, to be nibbled by the curious, the little
    cunners and toadfish that hunt these rocks. Bits cling to my
    ankles, a last quick embrace before the next wave carries you
    away.

Now you are gone, settling to mix with the white sand, the shining bits
    of mica, the blue fragments of mussel shell and the white
    fragments of clam, the pink and opalescence of mother of pearl.
    Turning and returning with the cycle of the sea.

This is the gift you have given me, Mother, this dream that sets you free.

Visitation

I wear my mother's skin, snug across my shoulders.

In this surprise visit, she shares my bed and my body. Her head nestles against my neck, cuddling to my left ear. Her silver hair is soft, comforting, like a toddler's favorite blanket. I sleep on my right side so I won't crush her against my pillow. When I look in the mirror, I see her face with mine, her blue eyes staring at me with their hawk stare.

The skin of her arms covers my arms, closely, warmly, her hands hanging above my hands like ruffles emerging from a sleeve. Her heavy breasts sag swinging from my chest. On my hips and legs, she is faded blue jeans, shrunk skintight. Her feet flop over my feet, fringed shoe-flaps.

When I was very young, I shared her bed sometimes, when we took our naps together in the big mahogany four-poster. Her broad, smooth back was toward me, her skin gleaming opalescent in the shaded room. I would nestle up to her, secure and comforted in her warmth, nesting like one silver teaspoon to another. Her body had its own faintly earthy smell, a smell that clung to her clothes, years after she had worn them. When we emptied her bureau drawers, I put on her blue cardigan sweater and pressed a blouse against my face, breathing the trace of her.

She loved to swim, and now we swim together in the warm, chlorine-scented pool in the old town she loved so well. Her body hugs mine beneath the bathing suit; her skin moves with mine. Her fingers and mine play pat-a-cake in the water; her feet and mine flip, frog-kicking.

After our swim, I take her to the mall. Everywhere, people crowding the bright promenade wear at least one skin besides their own. Some have two or three heads bobbing along beside their heads, eyes rolling sideways or straight up to the sky. People don't have to be dead to have someone else wear their skins.

Do the wearers even know the skins are there? Do the owners know someone is wearing their skin?

Hercules wears a lion skin, hide of his adversary, the Thespian terror. The great head hangs behind him, mouth open in a final fierce roar, eyes still staring.

But my mother is not my adversary. Once past the skirmishes of my adolescence, years ago, we made our peace, friends as well as family. She freed me as she could not free herself, for all her education and experience. Throughout her ninety-plus years, she judged herself by what she felt was her mother's judgment of her, always finding herself lacking.

My grandmother died when Mother was in her mid-thirties. In the final illness at home, Mother, my aunt, and a nurse cared for Grandmother. After her death, while my aunt and the nurse accompanied the hearse into town, my mother stayed behind to clean out Grandmother's bedroom. She was down on her hands and knees, in the closet, sweeping out the corners carefully, just as her mother had taught her. Suddenly, she told me, she felt her mother present, standing in the bedroom doorway. Mother went rigid, suspended, back in her girlhood again, awaiting condemnation. Her only thought was "What have I done wrong now?"

Then her mother was gone. "I thought later," Mother said, "that perhaps she had come back to tell me good-bye." But the visit brought no peace.

Mother was a social worker; she knew about carrying the dead weight of the past. "He can't get his father off his back," Mother would say of a client. Or of another, "She needs to get her mother off her back." She just couldn't heal herself. One of the last memories she let go, as her mind went on ahead of her, was the coal in her Christmas stocking the year she was seven. Her mother had decided she was selfish and greedy.

But negative images do not fit this visit. My mother is not weighing me down. Not a succubus straddling my shoulders and cracking her whip, making me stumble, panting, a two-legged pony in the race of life.

This visit feels like love. Why has she come, across the miles and the years? I study her face in my mirror, looking for answers. But the hawk eyes stare beyond me, blue as the vistas she is seeing, ahead on her long journey.

Now she is gone, as quickly and quietly as she came. She has flicked me easily out of the pod of her skin, flicked me with one thumb as though she were sitting in the sagging basketweave of the old green rocker on the screened back porch, shelling peas into a worn white-enameled colander on a June afternoon.

Freshly shelled, I glisten in the shadowy sunlight.

Charles

Charles (not his real name) sold ladies' underwear, door to door all through the 1930s. Unmarried. Lived with his mother. He had a regular route: farm wives and older women in the small towns around the seacoast—customers untouched by the revolutions of the Roaring Twenties.

He had gone to high school with my mother and my aunt. When Mother visited, he would stop by our beach cottage with his black sample case to demonstrate his latest lines, hoping, of course, that they would buy, though they never did. He would hold up to the sunlight the new peach-colored rayon with the wide, flaring legs, spreading his fingers inside the panties to show off the fabric. We had to look at bloomers, laid out on the dining room table. Cotton and rayon, pink and white. Ladies' knit undershirts unfolded, his careful hands smoothing the wrinkles over the bust. No corsets or brassieres; women fitters sold those. Charles showed his samples, took orders and deposits, delivered.

One summer, he announced he had a new (second-hand) car. He offered to take my cousin Nell and me for rides. We were eleven, just budding into puberty. Nell almost twelve, ahead of me, as she always was. No one raised a question. Everyone said, "That's nice."

We went on scenic drives, stopped to sight-see. Nell sat on the front seat, next to Charles. He looked like the movie actor Ralph Bellamy. We had fun.

On the third drive, we visited a small museum. I was on one side of the room, in front of a tall glass case. I could see Charles and Nell, reflected, standing together at an exhibit. He had his arm across her back, leaning toward her, pointing at something, whispering into her ear. I was jealous. "He likes her better than me."

When we got home, Nell disappeared. After Charles left, she reappeared, storming. "Charles touched me! He had his arm around me. I didn't know what to do. He felt the edge of my breast!" Almost crying.

Her mother laughed. "Poor Charles. Going after young girls. He wouldn't know what to do with a grown woman if he got one as a gift."

No one said anything to Charles, of course. That would have been embarrassing. And he was an old friend.

But the rides stopped.

James Francis Parnell

1884 -1963

My husband's father quit school after sixth grade
to work in the mills.
During the worst of the Depression,
Jim was foreman of an empty room, quiet machines.
On salary, not laid off like the hourly crew,
he went to work every day
to a mill that had no work.

Each morning, he went in, on time,
to the brick mill building behind his house
with his daily newspaper, his *Reader's Digest*,
Saturday Evening Post,
filling the time with reading.

At noon, he came home for dinner,
went back and read until quitting time.
Paid to be there, he was always there.

Evenings, he read his Bible.
At the last "Amen" of the Apocalypse,
he turned back to "In the Beginning..."

When the war came, business came back.
His room was the thread room,
where sheets of rubber were cut into elastic strips
to be woven into sock cuffs, belts, suspenders,
waistbands for pajamas and underwear.

Powdered soapstone
kept the rubber sheets from sticking together.
It sifted through the air in the room,
settled in dust on the tables and floors.
Jim brought the powder home on his clothes,
in his lungs.

A chest X-ray once, for an insurance exam,
showed great areas of white.
"What's that?" Jim asked, pointing.
His doctor laughed. "Jim, after all these years,
don't you know soapstone when you see it?"

He died at seventy-eight, congestive heart failure,
his coated lungs unable to breathe out the moisture
that was drowning him.

Bill says, "My father made $35 a week
while we four kids were growing up.
We lived in mill housing. Subsidized.
$10 a month for three bedrooms and a big yard.
I remember a neighbor's boy said to me once,
during the Depression, 'I wish our family
was rich like yours.'"

...Earth's the right place for love
I don't know where it's likely to go better.
ROBERT FROST, "Birches"

Boston Valentine

1947

I am leaning on the rough concrete parapet of the Mass. Ave. bridge over Comm. Ave., looking toward the Public Garden, waiting for you. We'll head for the Eliot Lounge, have a couple of drinks, listen to the piano player.

You are a silhouette walking toward me, too far away for me to see your face. I can pick you out of all the other dark shapes coming scattered along the sidewalk. I know you by the way you move. Amble, not stride.

Recognizing you, I am astonished by the sudden clutch at my entrails, the grabbing, hollow pain. A pain I remember. I am back in my high school days...watching the Sheriff of Nottingham capture Errol Flynn as Robin Hood...secretly scrutinizing Eric, the boy all the other girls like...sighing "Frankie!" when Sinatra sings "This Love of Mine."

You and I are engaged. This teen-age stuff is totally unexpected.

Until this instant, I did not realize.

I am—viscerally—in love with you.

Ritual

Every morning he wakes me,
gives me my first pill of the day,
placing it carefully in my open palm.
I pick it up, right thumb and forefinger,
place it in my mouth.
He hands me the cup
and I drink.

We both know.
Every gift given in love
is Eucharist.

Boundaries

We know how far we can go
in the double bed.
Know in our sleep
where the mid line
is in the old fourposter,
as though we are a long-ago
courting couple, proper lovers,
bundling
on a chill New Hampshire evening,
the coil of the courting candle
measuring togetherness.

Bill

His shoulders sag
with the weight of the wood.
Stooped forward more than usual
to keep his balance,
he quicksteps through the living room
heading for the woodstove,
worn black sneakers scuffing the carpet.

The rust-colored log carrier, stained leather,
hangs heavy from his left hand,
one last log grabbed in his right.
"Deep Peace" plays on the stereo.

His gray hair curls slightly
around the tonsure of his baldness.
He's wearing faded green jeans,
washed-out flannel shirt,
dark gray cardigan buttoned
against the cold of the woodpile journey.
He needs a shave.

The logs thump on the hearth.
He stacks each one exactly,
fitting it in its place in the iron log holder.
It's his third trip.
We'll sleep warm tonight.

Dark Necessity

for Ruth

Sister, do you remember?
When you were almost four, we went
for your first time, to visit at the beach.
All afternoon you played in the warm tide pools,
chasing the pink baby crabs, peeking, timid,
at the bigger ones, scarlet and cream,
dug backward into their sandy holes beneath the rocks,
claws tucked close, ready to snap.
You ducked away as those great red claws struck out
when the big kids teased with sticks.

That evening, you walked in your sleep—
remember the story the aunts loved to tell?
You stood crying at the top of the stairs.
"All the crabs. The crabs. The crabs."
Grownups rushed to you, reassuring,
held you, carried you back to bed,
stayed with you until the bad dreams were gone.

Now we gather to strengthen you
for this new nightmare journey.
You must pass alone with all your courage
into darkness. There you wander blindly, twisting
through the labyrinth of the netherworld,
its rough, lichened walls your only guide.
Your feet stumble on the rocky path.
Voices cry out around you
in untranslatable moans.
The damp air smells of blood.

At the nadir lurks
the giant malignant crab, stalked eyes glittering,
brandished claws gilded with phosphorescence.
The bubbles around his mouth

gleam in the dim light, oily rainbows.
You must fight him, this treacherous enemy,
elude his jagged pincers,
to return to the sunlight.

Sister, we wait here to welcome you,
emerging from your lonely journey.
Like Mother and the aunts,
we will hold you, reassure you,
sustain you with our love.

Ruth and Patsy

PAEAN: A Song of Celebration
Remembering the Growing-Up Years
for our sons: Bill, Ed, Larry, and Howard

Praise for
      cooking
      with its immediate completeness
            rare roast beef au jus with garlic and red wine
            crusty Swiss rosti potatoes, crisp and steaming
            creamy frozen chocolate cheese cake,
                  marbleized swirling
      all the teasing smells, textures, tastes.

Praise for
      laundry
      with the steam and the high soapy suds
      and the swishing agitation of the washer
      and the clean smell as I hang the wet clothes,
            shaken out,
      and the fresh soft feel of wind-drying.

Praise for
      ironing (yes, ironing!)
      with its hissing of steam and spray starch
      and its smells of warm cloth
      and the crisp smoothness to put away.

Praise for
      shining the silver and brass
      with the chemical pungency of the polish
      and the damp, gritty tarnish, black on the cloth
      and the soft, renewed gleam of the candlesticks
            and andirons and tableware.

Praise for
      needlepoint
      with its blending and contrasting patterns and colors

and its shapes that take shape as I work
and the stitches that stay in place
            when I put them there
and its perfection as a finished product.

Praise for
            our children, our sons
            with the wet, earthy smells of small boys
            and the appetites that appreciate
                        without saying thanks
            with the stains from living and growing
                        that can't be bleached away
            with their wrinkled, tumbled, busy lives
                        that won't be ironed flat and still
            with the gleam in their eyes and their spirits
                        burnished by their encounters with life
            with their shapes and textures that move and change
                        as they move and grow
            and their perfection as never-finished products
                        of their own shaping and making.

Legacy

We wanted her spayed. A young cat. Gray, sweet, a warm,
purring companion, just old enough for the surgery.

The vet said, "She's already pregnant." So young.
"We don't want kittens," we said. "That's fine," he said.
"We can do it now. No problem."

When we brought her home, she started looking for her
kittens, crying. The vet said, "Sometimes it affects them
that way."

She roamed the house, looking under beds, in closets,
under the sink. Pushing her way behind boxes in the cellar.
Crying.

One night we woke to a great crash. Rushing downstairs,
we found her, seven feet up, cowering on top of the wall
cabinets. She had knocked off the big punch bowl. Broken
glass everywhere.

A few days later, she disappeared. We put out food and
called her name. Posted flyers, advertised. The children
searched for her in all the nearby yards.

A neighbor said, "I saw her in the cattails near the creek at
the bottom of the lots. She was too fast for me."

Sometimes I think of her while I'm folding laundry or on
my knees scrubbing the bathtub. A gray shadow slips
among the creek weeds. Does she still search for the
kitttens? Or did she leave that memory behind with
memories of 9-Lives and our brand of love?

In my imaginings, she is not in a new home, not with another
family, far down the creek, with no reminders of her pain.

I never see her dead, though I know it's likely, victim of auto, coyote, or dog pack.

Instead I see her on her own, feral and free. No more pregnancies. All her shots. Even a flea collar. Free to rob nests, catch birds. Hunt mice and bugs, frogs and minnows. Free to find her own way. Choose her own bed, her own hiding place, a warm dry spot against the rain and cold.

Washing the dishes, I cut my finger on a shred of glass.

For Patrick

On learning that an adopted grand-nephew bears my name

Seven children, cousins ranged by height, stand on the lake shore. The rising sun throws long shadows behind them across the beach, adult shadows, shadows of giants. The cousins hold stones to skim across the water. The ideal skipping stone is round or oval, flat, smooth. One-quarter, one-half inch thick. The wrists snap and the stones skim, briefly kiss the water, rise, touch again, dragon-flies, swallows flying low.

Of all the skipping stones, hers flies the farthest, skims and touches, skims and touches, across the lake, over the trees on the opposite shore, into the dawn sky, out to the edge of infinity. No end to its flight, no end to the ripples that move ever outward.

Now her thrown stone turns, curving back over the intervening years, transformed. Flying saucer, space-sled. Its new-born rider clutches its sides with his long, wrinkled fingers, smiles his beige wrinkled smile. With him comes love, warm and radiant.

*The Lord made a covenant of friendship with him
and made him a prince....He preserved him for
his mercy...and made him blessed in glory.*

Within her a light always shimmered, a candle burning behind a white jade screen. Now, her face a star, she moves toward me, hands cupping a flame. Smiling, she holds out to me this shining gift, this child, this name.

(The quotation is from the liturgy for the Feast of St. Patrick)

Obsequies

"We have to have a funeral."

Chet's caterpillar is dead. Too much loving.
Too much holding in warm sticky three-year-old hands.
Poking with fat three-year-old fingers.

The four little girls, sisters and cousins, know funerals.
A great-grandmother two months ago.
A great-great aunt today.

Funerals are new dresses, dark printed cottons
that won't show grass stains,
spilled lemonade. Smears of chocolate.

Funerals are grassy hilltops. Flowers. Sunshine,
cloud-shadow. Breezes that tease the cotton dresses.

Funerals are a strange new word: inurnment.
Small, neat holes. Small, neat boxes
that fit in the holes. Flat stones with names.

Funerals are grown-ups talking. Telling stories.
Reading poems. Saying prayers. Serious, their voices
breaking a little sometimes, but they smile, too.
Even laugh a little, sometimes.

"He's dead. We have to have a funeral."

Natalie and Amanda, Hannah and Tasha,
still wearing their funeral dresses,
know what to do. Dig a small, neat hole
in the flower border. A box? A matchbox will do.
Find a flat stone. Someone to spell "caterpillar."

They let Chet come to the funeral. It was his caterpillar.
Services over, they crowd into the house,
looking for candy.

"We had a funeral, too."

for Liam and Sadie Claire

November 18, 1997

"This is a hand," you say,
pointing to a projecting squiggle
on the Rorshach image of the ultrasound.
"And this a face. See
the forehead and the line of the jaw.
And these," tracing vertebrae with a finger,
"are their spines."

Busy in their warm cave, the twins
construct themselves, forming
the intricacies of eye, the curving
fold of ear, the exactness
of fingers and toes.

Her fingers are long and slim,
like her arms, her legs.
Dancer... swimmer...
Stocky, robust, already
he flexes his biceps.
Soccer...football...baseball...
They mirror the family,
but they are themselves.

Born too early, they come
into a world not ready for
their incomplete perfection.
Twin shooting stars, they flash
across the night sky, then wink out,
leaving us earthbound,
staring upward into blackness.

EMILY: ...It goes so fast. We don't have time to look at one another....So all that was going on and we never noticed.....Good-by to clocks ticking ...and Mama's sunflowers. And food and coffee. And new-ironed dresses and hot baths...and sleeping and waking up. Oh, earth, you're too wonderful....Do any human beings ever realize life while they live it...?

STAGE MANAGER: No. (*Pause*) The saints and poets, maybe—they do some.

THORNTON WILDER, Act 5, *Our Town*

Moving Day

Mrs. Hermitcrab
slowly uncurls, withdrawing from the rooms
that no longer fit. Her stiff muscles ease
that have clung tight for so long.

The tenderness of her privacy
exposed to the cold currents, she
struggles forward, carrying underarm
her shoeboxes of dirt with
the chives she hopes will survive,
the coleus rooted for the move,
and the primroses, newly divided.
The moving van lurches ahead, loaded
with sofa, stereo, double bed,
boxes of towels, sheets, clothing,
the good china and glassware,
carefully wrapped.

Mrs. Hermitcrab wears five hats,
stacked high:
the last cartons were already filled.
Over her shoulder hangs her camera.
One claw clutches the cat carrier.

Arrived, she pokes her body, like an inquiring finger,
into the chambered maze, exploring backward, blindly,
measuring, touching, delicately, exquisitely.

Will the new space let her curl and settle,
filling the empty rooms with living?
In her purse is a can opener
and a can of cat food.

Translating from the Avian

On the telephone lines
this cold morning
birds group into words:

        one
        four two
        twelvetogether ten two
        six one eight

        the sentence
        the structure
        the poem

Peripatetic Author

According to our dog,

there is a story,
running serially
on every bush and every brick
and every branch
that we walk past.

He sniffs out each chapter
in dogged scrutiny,
then scribbles his own contribution

for the next installment.

The Poet and the Chocolate Rabbit

Writing a poem is like eating a chocolate Easter bunny.

In the beginning I tuck the temptation away at the back of
the closet shelf. It stands tall, like Alice's rabbit, taking a
watch from its waistcoat pocket. In the shadows its coat of
foil gleams blue, gold, and silver. I leave it there for a few
days, my mind turning it over and over, relishing the hidden
promise. I watch it slowly take shape in my thoughts,
discover itself.

Now I am ready to take a nibble at the poem, a lick here and
there. Pull back the foil to discover the sweetness, savor the
earthy scent.

Where to start? It makes no difference. Perhaps a bite or two
off the ears, the rich moisture slowing through me. Perhaps
its tail or its big bow tie. There are no rules for eating an
Easter bunny.

The pleasure centers of my brain twitch like a rabbit's nose.

I break open the poem as I break open the rabbit, joying in
its molded structure. It is a dark delight to leave and to come
back to, a succulent satisfaction during the day to know the
poem is hiding at home, its secrets waiting for me.

A time of crunching, a time of ruminating. Poetry friends
take their own nibbles, shaping the poem to their taste.

Finally, the last crumbs and I've polished it off. The old
rabbit is gone, that first glimmering vision, only a ball of
wrinkled foil left behind. In the rabbit's place is a finished
poem, tall and strong, in its own bright coat, its shining
language, ready to travel out on its own into the world.

Risk-takers

*In "Endymion," I leaped headlong into the sea, and
thereby have become better acquainted with the surroundings, the
quicksands, and the rocks, than if I had stayed on the green shore
...and took tea and comfortable advice.*

JOHN KEATS, 1818

She took tea and uncomfortable advice.

No headlong leap into the sea;
she knelt on the green shore of her garden,
a red blanket spread to keep the grass and earth
from her white dress.

She baked for a father
who would take bread
from no hands but hers

and once a year poured sherry for his guests.

Solitary she explored her surroundings,
the quicksands and the rocks,
scribbling her discoveries
on backs of envelopes,
scraps of paper—
paring, compressing.

And when word became diamond,
she copied into little books
tight-tied with string
and hid in her bureau

her letters to the world.

Two Spring Poems

I
Song for Anneliese

"Nature's first green," he said,
"is gold," thus preempting
for all other poets
the willow on your corner
in this thin spring sunshine.

II

Reprise

Against winter-empty branches
of slower trees,
the maples glow again.

This brief flowering,
russet-clustered,
reiterates autumn,
establishes April.

Millennium Messages

*I find letters from God dropt in the street,
and every one is sign'd by God's name.*
WALT WHITMAN

Torn paper flies in the wind,
parade confetti,
shredded memos,
red, gold, brown,
each bearing a scribble,
puzzles in God's handwriting.

If I hurry, run to gather them,
arms full, baskets full,
bring them in, spread them out,
diningroom table, basement floor,
can I jigsaw them together,
palmate and pinnate,
sawtoothed edge to sawtoothed edge,
color matching color?

Can I decipher them?
Before they fade and dry,
before they crumble,
will they reveal what waits for us
as the new year comes?

Tales Teachers Tell

The headline
appeals to the ninth grade prurience
of its reader (and probably to the
ninth-grade prurience
of the bored headline writer).
He sounds out the unfamiliar name:
"Virginia...uh...Pippa-lena
sets new record."

He needs "a current events story
to bring to class." This is good enough.
(He doesn't bother to read beyond the headline.)
And maybe he will shock the teacher,
a dream of ninth grade boys.
He never notices, or wonders why,
Virginia's story
is in the Business pages.

In class, he is first to raise his hand.
"I have a story about Virginia Pippa-lena,"
he says, and reads the headline:
"She 'sets new record. Laid by
240 men in one day.'"
The class giggles, and he smirks,
that ninth grade boy smirk.

The teacher knows ninth grade boys.
She says only,
"How do you spell 'Pippa-Lena'?"
and writes on the board
as he spells the name:
"P-I-P-E-L-I-N-E."

Fundamentals of Design

It's the first class. The art instructor picks up the sun-bleached cow skull she bought at a yard sale in Arizona, knowing at sight how she would use it.

Not speaking, she clicks the remote for the slide projector. The first image is a drawing, the female reproductive system, fallopian tubes stretching at right angles on each side, vagina partly cut away to show the ridged interior. The students murmur. This is art class, not biology.

She holds the skull up in the beam of light from the projector. Its shadow fits exactly over the drawing. Horns and fallopian tubes. Worn muzzle and vagina. Still not speaking, she moves the skull to one side, displaying both images. The next slide is Georgia O'Keeffe's "Cow's Skull —Red, White, and Blue." She flicks the slides back and forth without comment. Uterus. Painting. Uterus. Painting. And watching through empty eye sockets, the yard sale skull. Then she stops, quiet, looks at the class. Waits. Waits.

Finally, a first-year student raises his hand. Asks the question the instructor knows will always be asked.

"Do you think the artist did that on purpose?"

One Hundred Flowers

Georgia O'Keeffe
comes down River Road
to paint morning glories
on my neighbor's mailbox.
Heart-shaped leaves climb
the scarred paintcan base,
circle the metal post, green tones
lightening and darkening
with sun and shadow.

Only O'Keeffe's palette
could invent this blue,
slightly dusty like the sky
at the end of a cloudless summer afternoon,
but more intense, more glowing.
The ridges of each trumpet
are the palest possible pink;
one smidge of color less
and she would paint them white.
Thin bands of burning fuchsia
border the ridges. All lines lead
to the secret, shadowed center.

   "When you take a flower in your hand,"
   she tells my neighbor, *"and really look at it,*
   it's your world for the moment."

Lifting her brush
from the final finished blossom,
O'Keeffe watches her art
curl in the midday heat.
She will be back tomorrow
to paint more morning glories.

Reclining Figure *(Pablo Picasso, 1934)*

The room smells of paint and sleep and the lavender flowers
beside her bed. Her arms are smooth arcs, stretching
above her head, one elbow sliding slantwise from the sheets.
As if just awakening, she yawns in profile.
Her bare breasts turn toward the viewer,
giant rosy apples with green stem nipples.

The blue and white coverlet is bright, fresh,
as though painted this morning.
Under it, she tenses with delight, twisting
like a dancer, feeling her muscles obey.
Her buttocks, free of the tangled bedclothes,
repeat the curve of her breasts,
full and white, one cheek just touched with rose.

Her bent knees are covered; her bare calves
balance the outstretched arms.
Picasso catches the second of awakening, the yawning,
the supple spiraling and holding, before she relaxes.

This woman's warm flesh is dust now.
Or grown aged, withered.
I could not recognize her from her Cubist profile,
nor find her in an old photograph. But I know her.

My arms curving overhead, I mimic her,
torquing in her Cubist distortion.
I sense her strength, her energy.
I know her pride in holding this pose, her confidence
in the body she displays.

The curator finds aggression, torment, rape.
I feel no violence here to give me pain.
Just her pleasure in her round arms and legs,
her tiny ankles and feet, her full breasts and buttocks,
her pleasure in knowing she will be remembered
through the artist's eye,
feeling on her skin the thickness of the paint,
the sweep of brush on canvas.

Marfan Syndrome in the Brookgreen Sculpture Gardens

Pawley's Island, South Carolina

A head taller than any other visitor,
he walks the allée of liveoak and Spanish moss,
viewing the (strictly representational)
statuary.

Nothing here looks like him.

With his massive skull,
gnarled hands,
long arms, hunched back,
his immense dignity,
he is a Rodin burgher of Calais
beside the pert fauns, perky cherubs,
perfectly proportioned heroes.

Of all I see this afternoon
in Brookgreen Gardens,
only the concave planes
of his non-representational face
set my fingers sculpting
in clay of air.

Thinking Irish

Vignettes from an Irish Journal
Summer, 1993

"Have ye come
to claim your crown?"

•

On O'Connell Street
the uncrowned king:
"no...right to fix the boundary
to the march of a nation."
The gold harp of Ireland behind him,
his right hand outstretched,
pointing down Parnell Street
to the Parnell Pub.

•

Brian Boru, as predicted, died
at the Battle of Clontarf.
Today's battle of Clontarf:
buses, lorries, cars, motorcycles,
speeding down Clontarf Road.

•

Screenless windows open wide
to the insect-free Irish air. Patrick drove the snakes
from Ireland. Did he also drive out
flies and mosquitoes?

•

A hot water bottle, an aching back,
doorknob sign hanging,
the Sunday *London Times*.
A knock on the door.
"Did ye want to not be disturbed
all day long?"

•

Yeats sits in his tower
in a splayed wicker chair
trying to know the dancer
from the dance.

•

In the James Joyce pub in Limerick,
familiar caricature of Joyce fills one wall,
On another wall, the Joyce Tower.
On the corner T. V. —
rerun of "Falconcrest."

•

Once more unto the bus, dear friends.

•

On the golf links edging Galway Bay,
a ruined castle stands hazard
to the green.

•

There were nine children
in this West Cork farmhouse, two rooms,
a loft under the thatch, all ruins now.
Parents, the mother's mother, the father's mother,
the father's aunt. "Her family had all gone to
America. There was no one left to look after her."
The children slept in the loft, walked barefoot
to school, five miles away. A mile each way
for drinking water. Six miles to church each way,
twice a weekend: confession on Saturday, fasting
on Sunday. "We were happy."

•

Beyond the gravel works' piles of chippings,
beyond the stone barriers,
beyond the concrete breakwater with its
chalked slogan: "Brit troops out—support the IRA!"
beyond the rim of shoreline surf,
children swim in the Irish Sea.

•

The bales of hay are rolled in shining black,
marked in white, usually a cross.
"I HATE CROWS" reads one farmyard,
one letter to a bale, and down the road,
"CROWS ARE BASTARDS!"

•

In the photo of Mikey of Arklow,
the teeth of his jacket zipper
fall across his chest
like rosary beads

•

That Limerick poet, met in a Cobh pub,
told of his daughter, eight, and the bread bush.
She made balls of soft bread
and stuck them like flowers on a park tree. Birds
flew down and ate them—a bush blooming with birds.
In front of the blossoming, an oblivious man
sat and read his newspaper.
The editor gave the girl 1,000 Irish pounds
for rights to the photograph. He said.

•

Irish traffic jam: on the Ring of Kerry,
red-rumped sheep fill the road, oblivious,
grazing on the verge.

•

Hunkered in her niche in the window wall, Sheila-na-gig
glares into the hall of the great keep, reminding
entertainers in medieval gowns:
"Underneath your velvet, your lace and fake pearls,
underneath your makeup and your soft young flesh,
your singing and dancing,
I am what endures, the sinew, the bone, the strength."

•

Relic of the Neolithic, a standing stone,
inscribed in scratches of Ogham,
still stands erect in the green meadow,
a scratching stone for horses and cattle.

•

"Blarney Castle is bigger on the outside
than Bunratty Castle, but smaller on the inside.
Bunratty Castle is bigger on the inside than Blarney,
but smaller on the outside."
I am thinking Irish.

•

On the way to the airport, the young, earnest guide
talks of stabbings in Limerick, of knives
hidden in wall niches.
Behind her, through the windshield, glows a rainbow—
arcing above the Shannon road,
spilling its gold down the green hillside.

The Chieftains at the Music Hall
Portsmouth, N. H.
with a surprise appearance by James Galway

Sitting quiet in the balcony's half-darkness,
I dance:
>   body tenses for the held notes, pauses...
>   cadences rise to a suspended breath,
>   the catch in the throat of the grace note
>   the refrain, the dying fall...release

Each instrument plays me,
resonates my soul:
the plucked precision of the harp
twirling vibrato of the penny whistle
wordless voice of the violin
>   soaring, expiring, with the melody
Paddy Molony's uileann pipes
with their skirling banshee wail
muffled thump of the bodhran
>   drums of war, drums of death
>   drums of the dance

Galway, all breath and fingertips,
swirls me around the cherub trumpeters
of the proscenium boxes.
I grab for brass cut-out stars
glimmering in the ceiling's center.

Interrupting thunder of clogging:
stepdancers in synchronicity,
spotlighted in their black and white,
green and gold. Total decorum
above the waist; controlled abandon

of legs, feet. My feet, tapping with theirs,
can't match their rapid rhythmic beat.

Now Galway closes,
finding freshness in the familiar,
breaking our hearts
where we think we are immune.
We leave into the Portsmouth night,
grieving with a father
who bids his son farewell
so many wars ago.

Armistice

Remembering you
this Veterans Day,
I dig little graves,
little tombs and wombs.

Kneeling,
I trowel nine inches deep,
shaping hollow eggs
with shells of dirt,
add dark albumen
of compost, peat, manure,
and drop in
the tulip yolk,
closing all in darkness.

In spring, you will rise again,
heralded, not by red poppies
or purple flags of iris,
but by the hatching of the heart
in splendid banners,
scarlet, white, and gold.

Sanyu Mande, Uganda   *photo by Lisa Collins*
White Pines College, Class of 1990
   Sanyu fell ill in the spring of 1989. She returned to Uganda, where she died August 1, 1989. The College memorial service for her was held that September.

AFTER THE MEMORIAL SERVICE

Outside the chapel,
a black butterfly pauses on the sunny pathway,
spreading and closing its wings,
showing the tan border, the brown and yellow eyespots.
When I step forward, the wings take flight,
dance in the light air.

Sanyu, *Happy Child,* we tried to force you
into our patterns. Said "You must..." "You should..."
Laughing, you eluded us, finding your own way,
making us laugh in spite of ourselves,
surprising us with love.

Black butterfly,
We must not hold you here with our grief and guilt.
Opening wide our hands, we release you, Sanyu.
Now spread your wings, fly to new heights.
Our love goes with you as you learn your new world.

Bathroom Boehm

Mushrooms (toadstools?) grow
in my bathroom, a cluster sprouting
at angle of tub, wall tile, floor.
Found Art.
I have mopped with bleach, even
poured peroxide to kill the spores,
but the mushrooms keep coming back.

Opaque, ghostly white, a gray ring
banding the top: they are an art group
cast in the finest porcelain, somehow set
carelessly on the floor. Decorative Art.
If it were porcelain, it would have a bright
red-orange ladybug crawling on it.
Or a gnome napping beneath it.
Or a wee mousie perched atop.

I leave it alone, watch it grow.
Performance Art. The stems stretch up
as if feeding on the effluvium of a dead
hand. A Stephen King thriller. A corpse
hidden between floor and downstairs ceiling.

These mushrooms could be an illustration
in a children's book. Kid Art.
The occasional wasp, buzzing in around
the bathroom screen, could chew off
the largest one and fly away, using it
as an umbrella. The ants that somehow
find their way to the second floor could
take pieces back to their nest to feed their queen.

If it were marzipan,
I would eat it. Edible Art.
Or white chocolate, dusted with dry cocoa,
on a *buche de Noel*: a gourmet shop confection
scattering cinnamon spores on the bittersweet bark.

Moved four feet higher, it would be fine.
Horticultural Art.
Sitting on the window sill with angel-wing,
spider plant, pregnancy plant, mother in law's tongue.
With a sharp knife
I could dig out the cluster from its corner.
Transplant it. Tame it.
Teach it its place. Show it Nature is our property,
allowed to flourish only where we
let it live.

(Boehm Studios produce porcelain art in a variety of subjects: birds, flowers, Nativity sets, iguanas, polar bears, dolphins, cremation urns.)

Ecology Lesson

Sneezing, I reach for the box
of what I can't call Kleenex™
—that's not a generic word.
Call it "facial tissue,"
one of the 20th century euphemisms
that soak up bodily wastes.
"Don't put a cold in your pocket."
    Facial tissues   toilet tissues
    paper towels   paper napkins
    sanitary napkins   Handi-Wipes™
    disposable diapers   Swiffers™
all the trademarked "quicker-picker-uppers."
Words that consume our forests,
Everest our landfills, alter our landscapes
and our lives.

My mother, 70, 90 years ago,
used rags every month.
They were washed, bleached, and reused.
She said you could tell
by the neighborhood clotheslines
who was "on the rag."

With babies in our house,
cloth diapers soaked
in latrine-smelling diaper cans
until I drained them, rinsed them,
washed them in scalding water,
hung them to dry white
in the sunlight,
blown soft by the wind.
I had the whitest diapers on the block.

*DILEMMA: some experts say we use
more energy and cause more pollution by
doing laundry than by filling the landfills
with paper products.*

The soggy pyramids
of our disposable civilization
will last for eons at the dump.
Toilet paper overflows the sewer plants,
bobs in the harbor.
How many trees must fall
so I can blow my nose?

August 16, 1977

As I sit here
      straining

I see Elvis
      bloated body curled
            on my bathroom linoleum
      gold lamé pajama bottoms
            down around his knees.
He can't move his bowels.

Death does it for him.

Union Station, Washington, D. C.

Between trains,
I walked in the park
across from the white bulk of the station.
Thanksgiving weekend. A cold wind.
Trees black, bare limbs writhing
against the gray sky.

Few people on the sidewalk, but a man
came toward me. Tall, thin. Grayish-white skin.
A gray fedora pulled low
over his forehead. Hands in the pockets
of his long, worn overcoat, fusty greenish gray.
Just passing me, he flapped the coat open,
then quickly shut. What had I seen?

Something leathery-looking.
Maybe a camera in a brown case,
but hanging too low. I almost turned
to follow him and ask, "What was that?
I didn't get a good look."
Then I realized, and did turn.
Couldn't spot him anywhere
among the few people walking.
No police officer in sight, of course.
And what could I say if I found one?
Anyway, I had a train to catch.

Contemplating this man now, I marvel
at the strength of that compulsion,
driving him out, vulnerable,
into the punishing,
unforgiving wind.

When Slugs Have Sex

(Gardening Tip #103)

When slugs have sex
—giant slugs, six inches long—
they spin ropes of slime
out of themselves
and hang together from
tree bark or
the white wall
of our outside basement stairs.

Swaying slightly,
they turn themselves inside out,
iridescent, and press
their sexual parts together
in shuddering union.

Throw salt on them.

It sucks all
the water out of their bodies.
They die instantly
in simultaneous orgasm.

Do Angels Have Hairy Armpits?

"What Grace is Grace that's not known bodily?"
REX MCGUINN, "After the Dinner"

For the "creative expression" portion of the Women's Spirituality workshop, one participant brought in her painting of an angel holding up a mandala. The angel wore a skimpy tunic. Her breasts were large and firm; her arms were bare.

Everyone said, "What a beautiful angel!" I asked, "Why doesn't the angel have hair in her armpits?"

No one liked the question.

The artist looked confused. She said, "I never thought about it."

Well, let's think about it. Would an angel shave her legs? Pluck her eyebrows? Wax her bikini line?

No one in the Women's Spirituality workshop wanted to talk about angels and body hair.

Including me.

Lilies of the Field

Consider:

Winds have flung these weeds,
random order,
over the shoulders of the roadside,
over the piles of dirt
along the highway construction site.

Bindweed warp holds together
loose woven weft, nubby dark greens
lightened by goldenrod, chicory's blue sky,
feathery lavender of aster, Anne's royal lace.

Their design is circumstance.
No landscape architect
at a drawing board,
no highway engineer plotted them.

Yet Solomon in all his glory
had no garment rich
as this I rimple as my own.
I shrug the shaggy softness
over my shoulders,
wrap myself in the scent
of the living earth.

This robe will warm me
long after the road is done.

Of Trains and the Night and Rivers

The 2 a. m. freight train, heading north,
whistles its warning to river, marsh, and trees.
On this hot, still night, lying awake, all windows open,
I mark its coming by the sound.
Sometimes, when the wind is from the west,
the train leaps the track, wades the current,
rackets through our woods,
heading for Portsmouth Avenue.
Tonight, the train travels its own side of the Squamscott.
Steel wheels on steel rails click over the seams,
empty box cars clatter, more sharp bursts
of diesel whistle.

Not the steam whistle of my Virginia girlhood.
I am lying in bed, half asleep, listening to its cry,   .
the windows wide in the summer night.
On the far side of the James, the Norfolk & Western
heads toward the mines. Empty coal cars rattle.

Drowsing, I turn over in the narrow berth
of the Pullman car, swaying with its sway.
My wallet is tucked in the starched white case
covering the thin pillow.
My glasses inside my shoes
in the little green net hammock by my head.
Everywhere the sweet faint smell of coal smoke.

Stopped at a station, 2 a. m., we wait
for a new engine. I raise the green window shade
to a platform bare in greenish-yellow light. The station cat
watches from an empty baggage cart. A dark shape
in a railroad cap bustles by, lantern swinging.
With shouts, jolts, bangs, the new engine is attached,
and we roll, heading home. Picking up speed,
we cross the bridge to the dark countryside,
rumbling into sleep.

Memento Mori

Winter barrenness:
Last year's welcoming palms
are ashes now.

We, the walking dead,
move forward slowly, silently
under the yellow lights.

> *Remember that thou art dust*
> *and unto dust thou shalt return.*

Sealed   composed   isolate
we stumble slightly
finding our way.

In each forehead burns a black bullet-hole.
That empty third eye
gaping socket
looks into time
into self.

> *Remember that thou art dust*

Cross   Mark of Cain

We are killers   We are victims

Our deaths acknowledged,
we exit into the Lenten night.

At 92 my hand wraps around the pen
levels off in strength
for yet another day.

·

Poetry
healing energy,
saves one's life,
there, like the old squirrel
leaping branch to branch of a beech
tree, surviving, bark of life.

·

breathe deep
age disappears

ESTHER BUFFLER
"Fumes   late year 2000"
"Window"
"Med-Walker"
It's All Ahead

Cat Nap

Back in bed,
she flexes toward the foot,
feet finding the last
of the night's warmth.

The cat jumps beside her,
looking for love.

They cuddle,
dozing, until
the day
officially begins.

Hattie Miron
1894-2002

Coming home from your funeral, Hattie,
we stop at a garden shop.

You loved greengrowing life around you.
At the glass doors to your balcony,
plants stood tall on your living room floor,
hung in rows from the ceiling,
sat blooming on a long bench in the sunlight.

Driving past your building yesterday,
we saw only empty space
behind those doors.

In the shop I choose a goldfish plant.
The little orange flowers look like cheddar fish.
Pale green bracts are the fins and tail.
Tiny mouths open wide to gulp air.

The dark shiny leaves gleam wet,
like seaweed growing on rocks under water
with bright shapes darting
among the waving branches.

When we brought you communion,
you opened your mouth like these little fish.

I'll hang the plant in my dining room window
where it will catch the light.
You never lost your sense of humor.
I hear you laughing.

Once upon a Time...

At 2 a. m., the old woman
sits naked on the toilet
telling herself a fairy tale.
At happily-ever-after she rises.
Pauses.

"Did I take my shower?"

She can't remember.

Her skin is dry.
No clue there.

No fog on the mirror.

Ah!
Her shower cap is wet.

She grins,
grabs pajamas,
heads for bed.

Ariel at 60

The storytellers took away my voice
my identity
a sacrifice for human love
the Prince with the great dark eyes.

No happily-ever-after from
Hans Christian Andersen.
The pain of love
the pain of walking upright
and I was seafoam
immortal
daughter of the air.

Walt was sugar-sweet:
wicked sea-witch foiled
all problems dissolved
wedding bells.

Now I am human, 60,
the great sweep of hair grown gray
the firm flesh flagging.

A Queen in a bathing-dress
I swim on the surface with my sisters.
They will live to be 300—
they are still young.
Mermaids do not weep
but in their eyes I see their grief for me.

At night I slide into bed
as I slid through the sea-gardens of my childhood.
My legs a tail.
My feet flare into fins.
I smell the salt of my femaleness.

Deep in the cool recesses of the sheets
I bend and swirl, curling among the wrecked galleons.
Beside me the King sleeps
like an elephant seal,
galumphs, snores, a flipper over me in territoriality.

Three men have owned me
kept me voiceless.
Now I shall sing my own song
that all may hear my words.

Aphasiac

Tied in her wheelchair
in the sunshine of
the nursing home rec room,
she watches the lovers on the TV screen.
Their bodies speak to each other
in a language she no longer understands.

She and the other residents,
lined up together,
stare with empty faces
as if beholding Ibsen
in the original.

> *Once I knew that vocabulary,*
> *lived it, body to body. Tasted those nouns.*
> *Smelled them.*
> > *Moved with those verbs,*
> *motion without thought. Hands here,*
> *breasts, legs, there.*
> > *Touched those adjectives, just*
> *as they are touching. Relished the juiciness,*
> *like just-ripe cantaloupe.*
> > *Paced myself with those adverbs, speeding,*
> *slowing, dawdling.*
> > *Heard the lyrics that skin sings to skin.*

Now she sits through the love scenes
waiting for a commercial,
something she can name.
Toothpaste. Toilet paper.
This show has no subtitles
to help her remember.

La Leche

The bed clothes over her lonely shoulders,
crumpled together,
form a baby's head against her chest.
She buries her face in its softness.
The baby nudges her aging, empty breast,
mouth groping for the nipple.
She feels the sucking,
and her womb jumps, contracting.

Slow waves of warmth rise through her body.
She who is childless,
who has never nursed,
feels her milk let down.
The other breast fills to tightness,
and she finds another baby to nourish there.

Her milk is overflowing,
soaking her nightgown with its warmth.
Now she's at the lying-in ward.
"Do you need a wet-nurse?"

Rows of babies are not enough.
Her arms reach out in love
to all the hungry.
She could feed the universe.

She is Rose of Sharon,
huddled with the other migrants
in the rain-blackened barn, suckling
the starving,
dying man.

from the author...

Pat and Bill Parnell, Wallis Sands Beach, Rye, N. H.
photo by Debi Wheeler-Bean

According to my mother, I was writing poetry before I was old enough to remember writing it. She cherished a poem she said I had dictated to her when I was three.

Both my parents wrote. My father contributed to medical journals, articles like the one explaining how he had cured two young patients of stuttering by taking them off of all milk and citrus. (Allergies were one of his enthusiasms.)

Mother took creative writing classes at Virginia Commonwealth University, working with painful memories like her little brother stomping her Forget-me-nots or the coal in the Christmas stocking. She and I enjoyed putting together a book based on her "pen-pal" correspondence with an inmate in the Virginia Correctional system. Illiterate when they started, he learned to read and write so he could answer her letters.

All through school, college, and my own teaching jobs, I wrote (and edited) at every opportunity: school newspapers, yearbooks, literary magazines, even announcements for the P. A. system.

When our family bought the Journal Press newspapers in King George, Virginia, I became a contributing editor, sending in book reviews and food articles from New Hampshire and doing general reporting during my visits to my family. I appreciate the support of my sister and my niece, Ruth and Jessica Herrink, in publishing *Talking with Birches.*

A turning-point for my concepts of poetry came in an all-day workshop with William Stafford, then Poetry Consultant for the Library of Congress. "An idea comes and you write it down. It suggests another idea, and you write that down. When no more ideas come, the poem is finished." Over-simplifying, of course, but a liberating approach and great for teaching poetry.

In the summer of 1978, I participated in the first session of the Northern Virginia Writing Project, part of the Bay Area (California) Writing Project, with its emphasis on writing as a process, peer critiquing in writers' groups, and revision, revision, revision. Writers' groups have become an indispensable part of my writing process—seeing my work through the eyes of its readers—and I thank all those who have so generously given me the benefit of their insights, especially the poets of Skimmilk Farm, Brentwood, New Hampshire, who have been like members of a tough graduate seminar in the analysis and critiquing of poetry.

(For further information, go to www.patparnell.com)

Notes

The epigraph on p. 13 is from *Why the Woman is Singing on the Corner* by Dolores Kendrick (Peter Randall Publisher, Portsmouth, N. H., 2001), page 22.

The epigraph on p. 23 is from *The Secret Life of Bees* by Sue Monk Kidd (Penguin Books, London, England, 2002), page 107.

I found "rimple," p. 82, in a 1937 edition of *Roget's Thesaurus* as a synonym for "gather" and "fold." It is related to rumple, rivel, ruffle, wrinkle, crumple, crinkle, crankle. It means "gather into loose folds," the exact action I want for this poem.

The epigraph on p. 85 is drawn from three poems by Esther Buffler in *It's All Ahead* (Phineas, Portsmouth, N. H., 2003).

More Readers' Comments....

"The portrait of this woman [Min] of generations past is made more resonant by the handling of point of view, her story emerging out of family whispers and the observations of a participant observer."
—poet WESLEY MCNAIR, judging the Robert Penn Warren poetry competition, summer, 2000.

With a sharp ear for idiomatic speech and careful attention to authenticity, Pat Parnell has assembled a collection of narratives embodied with wisdom and humor. Emanating from the oral history of turn of twentieth century Virginia and the shores of coastal Maine and New Hampshire, these poems hold memory to the light of a dignified present. In *Talking with Birches*, the collective strength of women emerges in lessons of nature that both humble and empower as we are reminded, ultimately, of what keeps us all human.
—WALTER E. BUTTS, Dept. of English, Hesser College. Author of four collections of poems, including *Movies in a Small Town* and *White Bees*.

Pat Parnell's celebration of offbeat relatives and family acquaintances is touching and hilarious by turns. It reminds me of Gerald Durrell's classic, *My Family and Other Animals*.
—ELIZABETH KNIES, author of five collections of poetry including the most recent, *White Peonies*.

As vast and varied a landscape of plots and as kaleidoscopic a cast of characters as in any Dostoyevski novel. But Pat bests the Master in one important respect: her instincts lead her right to the life-sustaining humor in it all. We may never resolve what a good book is, but this is what a good book does.
—JOHN-MICHAEL ALBERT, poet, composer, singer. University of New Hampshire.